A Child's First Library of Learning

Music & Art

TIME-LIFE BOOKS • ALEXANDRIA, VIRGINIA

Contents

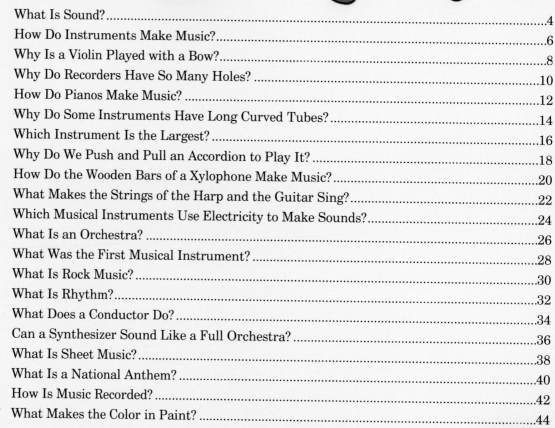

What Is Sound?

ANSWER Every sound starts when something shakes very fast. These quick little shakes are called vibrations. When a vibrating object shakes the air, the air moves in waves. When the waves reach our ears, we hear them as sound. Musical instruments send out sounds when we strike, strum, snap, scratch, pluck, or blow into them.

▶A sound makes the air around it vibrate. Sound waves move out in all directions.

▲We cannot see sounds as they move through the air. If we could, the sound waves would look like ripples in a pond when a rock is thrown into it.

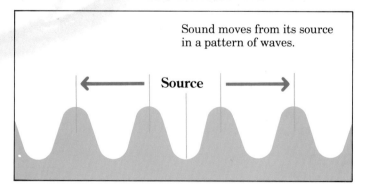

Sound moves from its source in a pattern of waves.

Source

4

■ Soft and loud sounds

When a sound is very soft, the peaks of the sound waves are low.

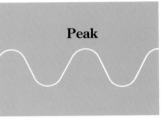

Peak

The peaks of the sound waves grow higher as the sound becomes louder.

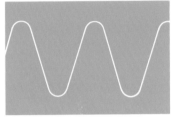

■ High and low sounds

When sound waves are close together and the distance between the peaks is small, we hear a high-pitched sound.

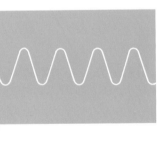

When the distance between sound waves is longer and the peaks are far apart, we hear a low-pitched sound.

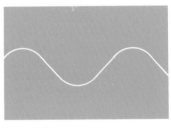

■ Tone

A violin and piano may play the same note but sound different. The special quality of each sound is called its tone.

? How Do Instruments Make Music?

ANSWER Instruments make music in several ways. Some have strings that vibrate when we touch them. Others make sounds when we blow into them. There are also instruments that musicians beat or strike.

▲ A harpist plucks a harp's strings to make music.

■ Stringed instruments

▲ A violinist draws a bow made of a wooden stick and hair from a horse's tail across violin strings.

▶ A piano sounds when hammers attached to its keys strike strings inside the instrument.

■ Wind instruments

▷ A flute is a small, hollow tube. When we blow across its mouthpiece the air vibrates and we hear a sound.

▲ To play a tuba, a musician puts his lips against the mouthpiece and blows.

■ Electric instruments

▽ Some instruments, like this electric guitar, use electricity to increase their sound or to change the way they sound.

■ Percussion instruments

A timpani can be tuned to make higher and lower pitches.

● To the Parent

Instrument classifications from the 19th century are still used. Stringed instruments produce their tone by vibrating strings. Woodwinds vibrate the air with a reed. Brass instruments sound from the players' vibrating lips. Percussion instruments sound when struck. Instruments that create a range of sounds and those that use electrical devices are classified in the newer categories of keyboard and electronic instruments.

7

? Why Is a Violin Played with a Bow?

ANSWER A violin is not strummed like a guitar or plucked like a harp. Instead the player moves a bow across the violin's four strings. As a result, the instrument produces a gentle sound. By changing the way the bow is used, a violinist can make beautiful melodies.

■ Played with a bow

Four instruments in an orchestra are played with a bow. From smallest to largest, they are the violin, viola, cello, and double bass.

▲ One of the first stringed instruments ever made was the lyre. Players plucked its strings to make music in ancient Sumer long before the violin was invented.

▲ A bow is made of a wooden stick and 200 hairs from a horse's tail. The rough hairs pull at the violin's strings.

Which Instrument Came First?

No one knows for certain how the violin was invented. Instruments like it have existed since ancient times. One of the first stringed instruments to be played with a bow was the *rabaab* of Iran.

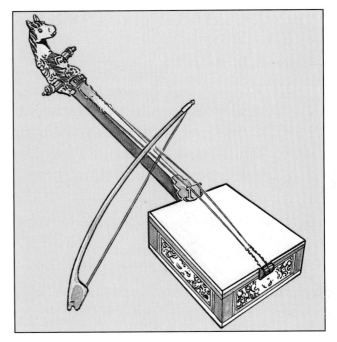

▲ The *rabaab* was brought from Iran to Mongolia. There it went through some changes and later became known as the *batookin*.

▲ The *rabaab* had the same basic shape as a violin and was played by drawing a bow across the strings.

▶ The *rabaab* led to the development of an instrument called a rebec in Europe. The violin came along in about 1550.

● **To the Parent**

The violin may be the best known of all Western orchestral instruments. Although its exact origin is uncertain, the violin seems to have developed in Europe from bowed instruments such as the rebec and the lira da braccio. The basic design of the violin has changed little since the early versions were built more than 400 years ago.

Why Do Recorders Have So Many Holes?

ANSWER Recorders have many holes to sound different notes. When we cover all the holes, the sound has to travel far through the instrument. Then the note that comes out sounds low. The fewer holes we cover, the higher the note.

■ Playing the recorder

When we blow into a recorder, the air comes out of the open holes. The pitch of the notes depends on which holes are blocked and which holes are open.

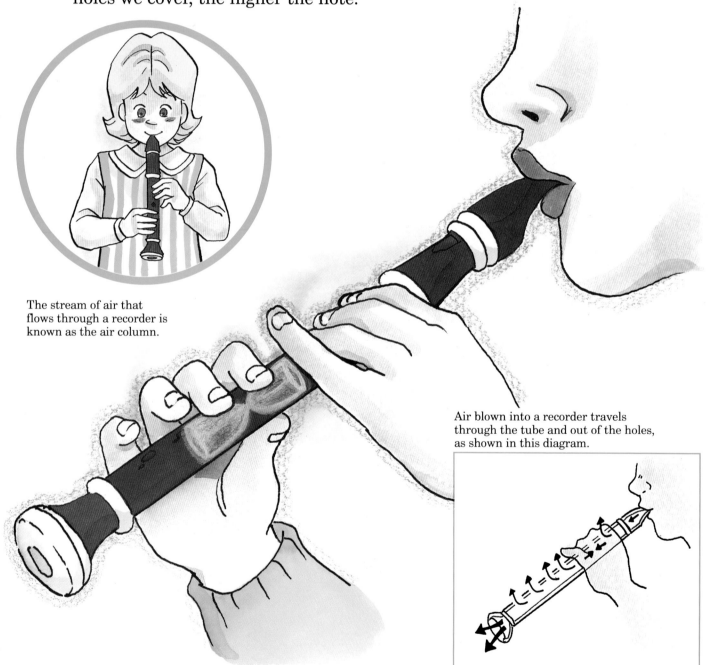

The stream of air that flows through a recorder is known as the air column.

Air blown into a recorder travels through the tube and out of the holes, as shown in this diagram.

■ Changing the length of the air column

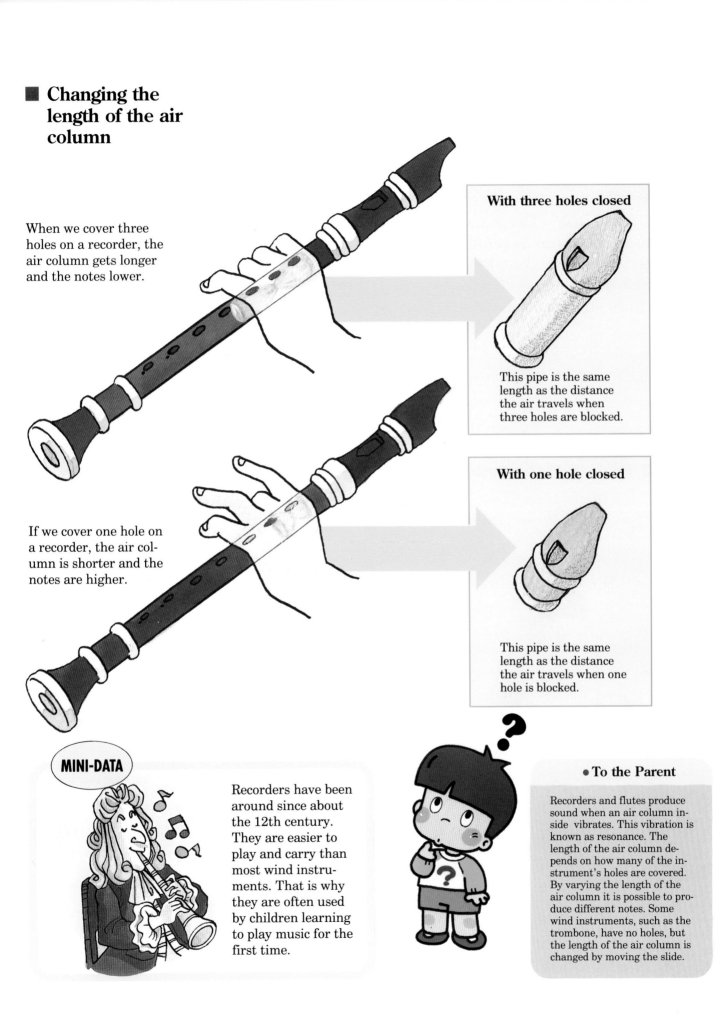

When we cover three holes on a recorder, the air column gets longer and the notes lower.

With three holes closed

This pipe is the same length as the distance the air travels when three holes are blocked.

If we cover one hole on a recorder, the air column is shorter and the notes are higher.

With one hole closed

This pipe is the same length as the distance the air travels when one hole is blocked.

MINI-DATA

Recorders have been around since about the 12th century. They are easier to play and carry than most wind instruments. That is why they are often used by children learning to play music for the first time.

● To the Parent

Recorders and flutes produce sound when an air column inside vibrates. This vibration is known as resonance. The length of the air column depends on how many of the instrument's holes are covered. By varying the length of the air column it is possible to produce different notes. Some wind instruments, such as the trombone, have no holes, but the length of the air column is changed by moving the slide.

? How Do Pianos Make Music?

ANSWER Every piano key is attached to a small, felt-covered hammer. When we play a key, its hammer strikes one or more strings inside the piano and makes a musical sound. A piano has many more strings inside than keys on the keyboard outside. Some keys strike two or three strings at once.

■ History of the piano

2 The clavichord was a favorite instrument from the 15th to about the 18th century. It has a keyboard and wooden hammers that strike the strings.

1 Several stringed instruments were popular before the piano was invented. The dulcimer was first used in Europe in the 15th century. The player strikes its strings with two wooden hammers.

4 By the 19th century, the harpsichord lost popularity because it did not produce loud and soft notes well. The pianos were shaped like modern grand pianos.

•To the Parent

The modern piano has two basic designs: the upright version played in homes and the grand piano of concert halls, where its open lid helps project sound. Because of the way it produces sound, the piano is classified as a percussion instrument in some countries and as a stringed instrument in others.

3 The harpsichord, which was invented in the 16th century, has a key for each of its strings. When a key is pressed, its string is plucked, not struck by a hammer.

■ Harpsichords and pianos

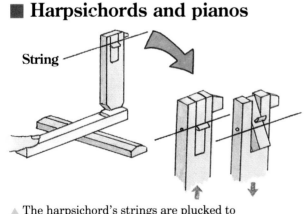

String

▲ The harpsichord's strings are plucked to make sound. It can't play soft or loud notes well so it is not suited to a large orchestra.

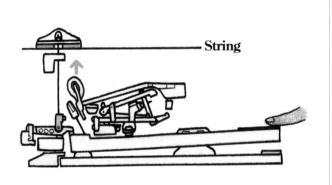

String

▲ Hammers strike a piano's strings. Depending on how hard the keys are pressed, the sound may be loud or soft. A piano can be played alone or as part of an orchestra.

❓ Why Do Some Instruments Have Long Curved Tubes?

ANSWER Brass horns are wind instruments. They have long tubes for making sounds. The longer the tube, the wider the range of notes it can make. Wound in a coil, the instrument is easier to hold and to carry.

■ The history of horns

2

By the Middle Ages, horns became longer, but most were not as large as the alpenhorn above. They could make more notes but were harder to hold.

1

The first horns were made from animal horns and blown by herdsmen calling livestock. Hunters and watchmen also used horns to call each other or to sound a warning.

3

During the 17th century, metal horns were curved and fitted with a tubular mouthpiece so it was easier to make different notes. But there was a limit to what a mouthpiece could do and how far a horn could curve. A removable ring of tubing was put inside the outer ring of some horns to increase high and low notes' range.

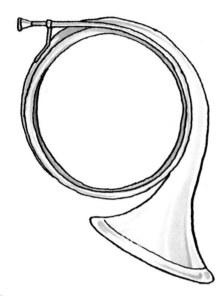

4

In the early 19th century, horns were fitted with valves. The valves switch between two sets of coiled tubing and make it unnecessary to add or remove the inner ring. Pressing the valve stops increases the length of the tubing .

■ Horns and butterflies

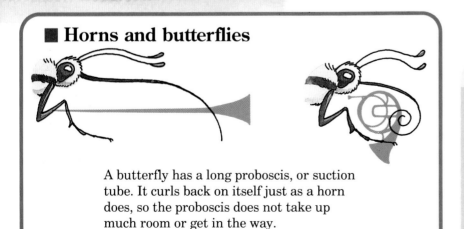

A butterfly has a long proboscis, or suction tube. It curls back on itself just as a horn does, so the proboscis does not take up much room or get in the way.

●**To the Parent**

Early horns were used for calling livestock, organizing hunts, or signaling soldiers in battle. Today's more versatile brass instruments are curved tubes with a mouthpiece on one end and a bell-shaped opening on the other. Trombones have tubing that slides to change their length and play different notes. Trumpets, French horns, and tubas share one basic design. They have three lengths of tubing that are controlled by three valves.

? Which Instrument Is the Largest?

(ANSWER) The pipe organ is the largest instrument. It can have thousands of pipes. In spite of its size, it makes music much as a simple recorder does. An organist uses keyboards and foot pedals so air flows through the pipes to make a tone.

▼ A pipe organ has keyboards and pipes. Its sound fills large places such as churches and concert halls.

▲ An electric organ makes sounds from electric impulses instead of from air moving through large pipes. Like a pipe organ, it often has many keyboards and pedals.

 # Can Feet Play Music?

A large pipe organ has many keyboards that keep a musician's hands busy. To play all the notes, she must also use her feet. An organ has foot pedals, called pedal boards, that are used to play some of its lower notes. An organist wears special narrow shoes to push the wooden bars on the pedal board.

■ The musical range of different instruments

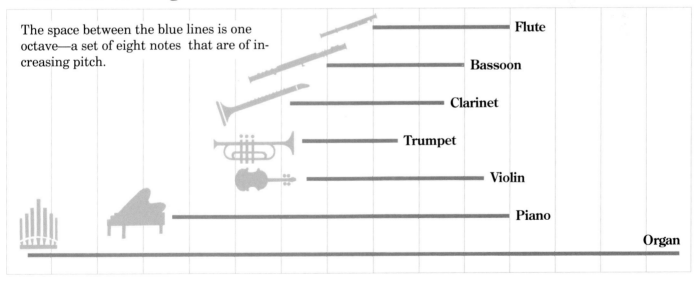

The space between the blue lines is one octave—a set of eight notes that are of increasing pitch.

Flute

Bassoon

Clarinet

Trumpet

Violin

Piano

Organ

Instruments produce different ranges of pitch. A pipe organ's pedals help extend its range. As a result it produces an extremely wide range of pitches from low to high.

● **To the Parent**

Bellows pump air into an organ's pipes. When the organist presses keys, air enters the pipes from a windchest between the keys and the pipes. Tones form as the air is forced through a hole in the pipes. Organists achieve different effects by adjusting the knobs and levers, called stops, located around the keyboards. Some organs use more than 10,000 pipes to produce music of great power and tonal variety.

❓ Why Do We Push and Pull an Accordion to Play It?

ANSWER The middle part of an accordion is called the bellows. As we push and pull the bellows, air goes into and out of them. The air flows over metal reeds that vibrate to make sounds. Accordions are played with a keyboard and finger buttons. The keyboard plays the melody, and the buttons play the chords, which are the sounds made when three or more notes are played together.

■ Playing an accordion

A player holds an accordion against the chest. To support the heavy instrument further, the player wears straps that go over the shoulders and down the back. The bellows, which are pushed or pulled to force air through the instrument, control the volume.

■ Harmonica

The harmonica is another instrument that produces sound when air causes the reeds inside to vibrate. The player presses his lips to the mouthpiece and blows air in or draws it out.

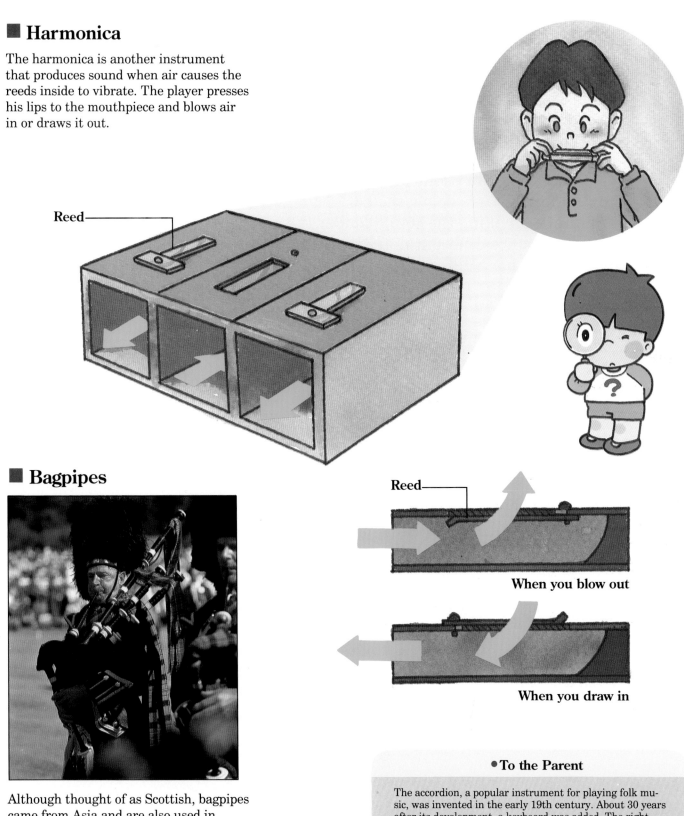

Reed

Reed

When you blow out

When you draw in

■ Bagpipes

Although thought of as Scottish, bagpipes came from Asia and are also used in Ireland and other parts of Europe. They have two or three reeds mounted on each bag of sheepskin or goatskin. Air from the bag is forced through the reeds.

● **To the Parent**

The accordion, a popular instrument for playing folk music, was invented in the early 19th century. About 30 years after its development, a keyboard was added. The right hand plays the melody on the keyboard while the left hand works the bellows and plays chords with the finger buttons. The number of finger buttons can range from 24 to 140, with 120 considered standard. The sound is produced by reeds inside the instrument that differ in shape, density, and elasticity. The flow of air across different reeds determines the pitch.

How Do the Wooden Bars of a Xylophone Make Music?

ANSWER A xylophone consists of rows of wooden bars set on a frame. When a player strikes a bar, its vibrations make a sound. A hollow tube below the bar also vibrates, making the sound louder. The bars produce different notes because they all have different lengths.

■ Playing a xylophone

To play a tune, a player strikes the bars with sticks or mallets.

▲ When the player strikes a short bar, the xylophone produces a high note.

▶ When the player strikes a long bar, it sounds a low note.

■ Percussion instruments

The children in the choir shown above are ringing hand bells. Each bell produces a single note. To play a song, a bell choir needs many hand bells.

Several of the percussion instruments in the illustration above are related to the xylophone. The instruments are from the country of Indonesia and are used to play traditional Indonesian music.

■ One-note instruments

Each of the percussion instruments shown below and at right makes only a single sound. These instruments cannot be used to play songs. They can only add rhythm to music.

Tambourine

Cymbals

Triangle

•To the Parent

Percussion instruments are of ancient origin and have played an important role in many cultures. In general, percussion instruments fall into two categories. The xylophone is an example of a percussion instrument that can be tuned to produce a range of pitches. Other members of this family include the marimba, glockenspiel, and vibraphone. Instruments in the second category cannot play melodies but produce only a single note. These so-called unpitched percussion instruments include the drums, tambourine, cymbals, castanets, maracas, and triangle.

What Makes the Strings of the Harp and the Guitar Sing?

ANSWER The harp and the guitar make sounds when their strings vibrate. Strings can be long or short, thick or thin, and loosely or tightly strung. All of these things change the sound of a string. The different sounds can be combined to play beautiful melodies.

▼ A modern harp usually has 47 strings. Each makes a different sound. Harps play both single notes and groups of notes called chords.

■ The harp

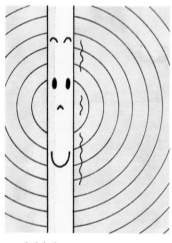

The strings of a harp come in different thicknesses and lengths. The strings nearest the harpist are shorter and thinner. The harpist plucks these strings to produce high notes. The longer, thicker strings make low notes.

▲ **A high note**

▲ **A low note**

▲ **A medium note**

■ The guitar

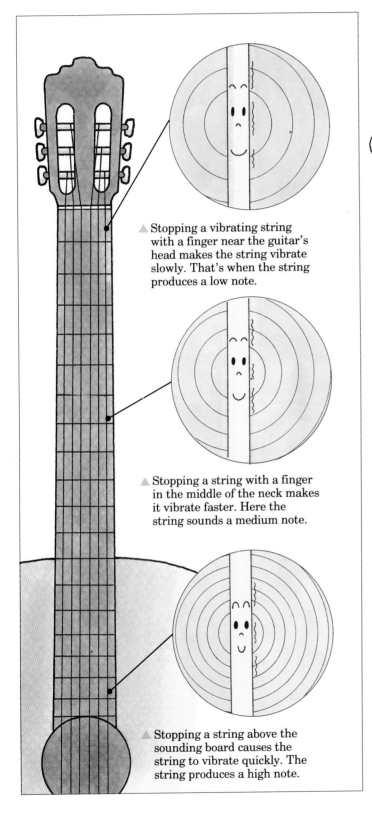

▲ Stopping a vibrating string with a finger near the guitar's head makes the string vibrate slowly. That's when the string produces a low note.

▲ Stopping a string with a finger in the middle of the neck makes it vibrate faster. Here the string sounds a medium note.

▲ Stopping a string above the sounding board causes the string to vibrate quickly. The string produces a high note.

▲ A guitar usually has six strings. A player strums the strings with the thumb or fingers of one hand, while stopping the strings with the other hand.

● To the Parent

Stringed instruments make different notes depending on the length, tension, and thickness of their strings. Many can produce subtle variations of melody and harmony. A harp's tones can be raised or lowered half a note by using the foot pedal. A guitar's sound is varied by using a finger to stop the strings at different points along the neck or by adjusting the tension of the strings with tuning pegs in the head. The guitar's sound is amplified when the strings' vibrations travel to the instrument's hollow soundbox.

Which Musical Instruments Use Electricity to Make Sound?

(ANSWER) Most instruments produce sound by making the air vibrate through blowing or strumming. A few, however, use electricity to make sounds. Two popular electric instruments are the guitar and the synthesizer.

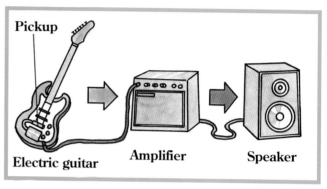

Pickup

Electric guitar   Amplifier   Speaker

■ Electric guitars

The strings on an electric guitar are made of metal instead of nylon. Below the strings are tiny microphones called pickups, which convert sound waves into electrical signals. When the strings vibrate, the pickups send electrical signals through wires to the amplifier. There the signals are made stronger. Next the signals go to a speaker, where they are converted back to sound waves so we can hear them.

■ Wired to make sound

▲ Electric guitar

▲ Electric drums

▉ Modern instruments

Electronic instruments do not make their
own sounds. They have computer chips inside
them that produce the many different sounds
played by the keyboard. The electronic signals
go from the computer chip to an amplifier
and then to a speaker to be heard.

▲ Electronic piano

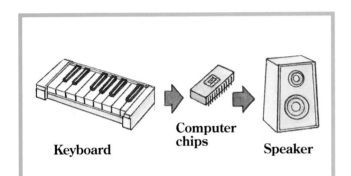

Keyboard   **Computer chips**   **Speaker**

▉ Synthesizer

An electronic synthesizer looks like an electric organ because it makes sounds from a
keyboard. Because of its computer memory, a
synthesizer can be used to play many sounds,
as if it were an entire orchestra or choir.

▲ Remote keyboard

● To the Parent

All traditional musical instruments produce sounds by making the air vibrate. With the advance of new technology, electricity has been able to produce sound signals that imitate a
wide range of music. The first electric guitars, organs, and
pianos have been followed by ever more sophisticated devices
that make use of rapidly advancing computer technology.
Modern synthesizers can reshape sound waves and so can
copy the pitch and tone of any orchestral instrument. They
are also able to create electronic sounds beyond the capabili-
ties of conventional musical instruments.

? What Is an Orchestra?

ANSWER An orchestra is a group of musicians playing on stringed, woodwind, brass, and percussion instruments. The orchestra can vary in size from 10 to 100 players. Composers write music that beautifully blends the sounds of these different instruments.

■ The parts of an orchestra

Orchestral instruments play different roles. Sometimes only certain groups of instruments play. Other times a single musician may play alone. Because stringed instruments most nearly mimic the sounds of people singing, they often play the melody while other instruments play harmony.

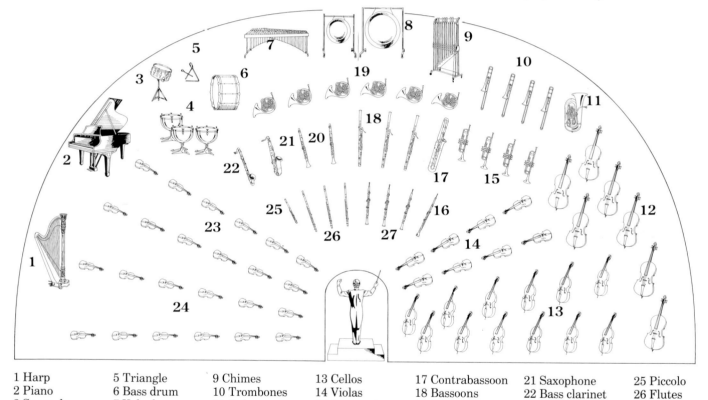

1 Harp	5 Triangle	9 Chimes	13 Cellos	17 Contrabassoon	21 Saxophone	25 Piccolo
2 Piano	6 Bass drum	10 Trombones	14 Violas	18 Bassoons	22 Bass clarinet	26 Flutes
3 Snare drum	7 Xylophone	11 Tuba	15 Trumpets	19 French horns	23 Second violins	27 Oboes
4 Timpani	8 Gongs	12 Contrabasses	16 English horn	20 Clarinets	24 First violins	

The National Symphony Orchestra performs with conductor Mstislav Rostropovich at the Kennedy Center in Washington, D.C.

■ History of orchestras

◀ Long before there were orchestras, the people of ancient Greece gathered in theaters to sing and play musical instruments. The Greeks also formed choruses that sang and danced during plays. The place where they performed was called the orchestra. Today the word is used to describe the people and instruments that play there.

▶ Beginning in the 1600s, opera became very popular in Europe. An area was created between the stage and the seats for the audience. The musicians who played for the opera singers sat in this area. This came to be called the orchestra pit.

▼ By the late 1700s, the Austrian composer Franz Joseph Haydn created the arrangement of the orchestra's instruments much as we know it today.

❓ What Was the First Musical Instrument?

ANSWER Percussion instruments probably were the first instruments people ever used. Long ago, people beat pieces of wood or other objects together to make sounds and then enjoyed the rhythm.

▶ Even in the earliest times, people expressed happiness by clapping their hands or stamping their feet.

■ Ancient percussion

▲ In ancient Egypt, the *krotala* was an instrument made of wood or ivory. Played with both hands, it worked like castanets.

▲ Drums were made long ago when people stretched animal skins over a frame made out of wood.

▲ The basic idea of the xylophone took shape when ancient people lined up rows of sticks and hit them with another stick.

■ First stringed instruments

▲ When early people shot arrows, their bow string would vibrate and hum.

■ First wind instruments

Wind instruments are nearly as old as percussion instruments. The first ones were made of reeds, animal horns, and shells.

▲ Later on in ancient Greece, bow strings led to the development of the harplike lyre.

Shell horn

Animal horn

Reed flute

■ Many pipes

The panpipe is a kind of flute. It is made from reed pipes of different lengths. Panpipes may have been the forerunner of pipe organs.

● **To the Parent**

Musical instruments have been around since prehistoric times. There is no record of their origin. Ancient people must have observed how things, such as hollow tree trunks and hunting bows, produced sounds when struck or plucked. The first true musical instruments were probably stringed. More refined percussion instruments and wind instruments made from reeds also date from the distant past.

? What Is Rock Music?

ANSWER Rock-and-roll music got its start in the early 1950s in the United States. The sound grew from other popular American styles of music. The main instruments of rock-and-roll are electric guitar, bass guitar, and drums. The music became a favorite of young people and spread around the world.

▲ In rock music, drums keep a loud, steady beat. A lead guitar plays the solos, and a bass guitar pumps out a driving bass sound. Some bands also use electric keyboards, a saxophone, or other instruments.

■ Rock music superstars

Chuck Berry was one of the first musicians to play rock-and-roll in the early 1950s. A few years later Elvis Presley became this music's biggest star. Four young Englishmen known as the Beatles made rock-and-roll a worldwide craze in the 1960s.

▲ Elvis Presley

◀ Chuck Berry

30

■ Roots of rock music

▲ Country music grew out of the ballads brought to the United States from England, Ireland, and Scotland. Artists like Elvis Presley grew up listening to this type of music.

▲ Rhythm-and-blues was the most important influence that led to rock music. This form of music was first played and performed by African Americans.

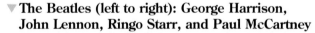

▼ The Beatles (left to right): George Harrison, John Lennon, Ringo Starr, and Paul McCartney

● To the Parent

Rock music grew out of a variety of musical traditions in the U.S., including rhythm-and-blues and country-and-western music. Because of its powerful beat and the simple urgency of its lyrics, rock music instantly became popular with teenagers. The first rock record, "Rock around the Clock," was produced by Bill Haley and the Comets. Haley succeeded by taking the intense power of African American rhythm-and-blues and making it accessible to a larger audience.

What Is Rhythm?

ANSWER Rhythm is one of the basic parts of music. Every song follows a regular pattern. When you clap your hands to the music, you are following the rhythm of that song. In a song, rhythm repeats a pattern of loud and soft, or strong and weak.

■ Follow the beat

Sing a song and clap your hands. Can you follow the rhythm? Can you hear whether the beat is strong or weak or whether it is fast or slow? Now try again with a different song, and hear how the rhythm changes.

■ Rhythm makes music fun

And What Is Melody?

Every song has a different tune. It is the way the high notes and low notes, short notes and long notes all fit together. This is called its melody. When you sing a song, the words follow the song's melody.

■ Musical glasses

1. Take at least eight glasses or jars that are exactly alike.
2. Add a little water to one glass. Tap it with a spoon. Find the same note on a piano.
3. Add more water to the next glass to make the next lower note on the musical scale. Do this with all the glasses to get a range of sounds from high to low. Now can you play a tune?

①

②

③

•To the Parent

Rhythm is a pattern that gives regularity to something interconnected and repetitive. Rhythm refers not only to the repetition of strong and weak beats but also to such things as high and low sounds. Rhythm is hard to explain to children since they cannot see it. It may be helpful to clap your hands in a simple rhythmic pattern. Even young children can hear the pattern and copy it. You can then have them use their hands to pick out strong-weak and high-low beats of a song they know.

What Does a Conductor Do?

(ANSWER) An orchestra has many instruments with different parts to play. A conductor makes sure that each musician plays his or her part correctly. The conductor uses a stick called a baton to show the beat and to help the orchestra members play with feeling.

■ The conductor

The conductor moves a baton to mark the rhythm of the music. The drawings at right show how the baton moves. Each conductor has his or her own way of getting the musicians to play faster or slower and louder or softer.

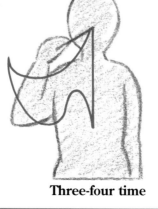

Three-four time

Four-four time

■ History of conducting

A conductor's job is an old profession. Even in ancient Egypt more than 3,000 years ago, a person playing a musical instrument would watch a conductor.

The first orchestras in 17th-century Europe had two conductors. One was a keyboard musician. The other conductor was one of the musicians playing stringed instruments.

When keyboard instruments were dropped from the orchestra, only one conductor remained. That person was chosen from the musicians playing stringed instruments and used a bow as a baton.

In time the conductor was often the composer of the music being played.

Later conducting became a full-time job, and the composer only wrote music.

Can a Synthesizer Sound Like a Full Orchestra?

ANSWER A synthesizer can sound like any instrument. When the player presses a key to mimic a particular instrument, electricity produces a signal of a certain pitch. Then the signal is changed to sound like the chosen instrument. Finally the signal is played as the music we hear. A synthesizer can combine and play sounds that copy many instruments at once so that it will sound like an entire orchestra.

■ How it works

When a player presses the keys on a synthesizer, electrical signals of a particular pitch, tonal quality, and volume are created by the computer inside it. The signals can then be stored or played from speakers as sound.

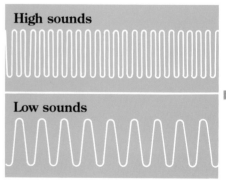

High sounds

Low sounds

▲ When the musician presses a key, the synthesizer emits an electrical signal that corresponds to a particular sound.

■ Playing a synthesizer

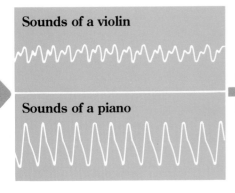
▲ Two or three synthesizers can be played at the same time or with regular instruments.

■ Sampling

The human voice or any other sound can be fed electronically through a microphone into a synthesizer and played back. This is called sampling. Sampled sounds can even be reshaped and changed and then played as new sounds.

Sounds of a violin	Loud sounds

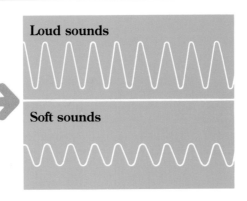

Sounds of a piano	Soft sounds

▲ The musician can program the synthesizer to play the note as it would sound if it were made by a particular instrument.

▲ Signals are then sent to an amplifier and from there to speakers to be converted into music. They can also be recorded directly onto tape.

● To the Parent

The synthesizer, which was invented in the 20th century, is one of the musical wonders of the modern age. It has five basic parts—a signal source that creates electrical flow, an analog or digital modifier that changes signals, a keyboard system that controls operations, mixers that combine different signals, and an output system that amplifies and plays sounds.

What Is Sheet Music?

ANSWER Sheet music shows in notations on paper how a song is supposed to be played. Each note tells how high or low the musical sound should be. This is called the pitch. The notes also show how long each sound should last. This is called the timing. When an orchestra plays a melody, each instrument has its part written on a piece of sheet music.

▲ Music was popular in the earliest times. A person passed on a song by teaching another person to play or sing it. There was no way to write music.

■ History of sheet music

▲ The Egyptians first wrote music more than 3,000 years ago. Their sheet music showed notes but no rhythm or chords. This musical manuscript is an Egyptian song in praise of love.

▲ This early sheet of music was written in Italy around the year 800. The flowing lines show the rise and fall of the melody.

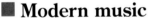 This ornamented sheet of music shows a German hymn from the year 1200. Square and diamond-shaped notes were written on a four-line musical staff.

▲ Around the 18th century, sheet music looked much as it does today. Notes are written on a five-line staff, indicating pitch and timing. This sheet is from a work by German composer Johann Sebastian Bach.

■ Modern music

Composers of modern music sometimes use nontraditional symbols to show how the music should be played. For example, diagrams like those in this picture may represent a tune. And today, computers are sometimes used as a tool in composing music.

❓ What Is a National Anthem?

(ANSWER) Music is important to all people. Most countries have a special song to praise their nation. The song is called a national anthem. When people hear that song, they feel proud of their country.

■ The French anthem

The national anthem of France is called "La Marseillaise." The song was written 200 years ago during the French Revolution.

■ The Chinese anthem

The song "Yi Yong Jun Jing Xing Qu" was written in the 1930s when China was in a war against Japan. The fighting song became so popular, it was later chosen as China's national anthem.

■ The United States anthem

Francis Scott Key wrote the words to "The Star-Spangled Banner" in 1814. He began writing the poem while watching British ships attack Fort McHenry in Baltimore, Maryland. The poem was later set to music.

? How Is Music Recorded?

ANSWER Anytime we want to listen to music, we can play a CD, a record, or a tape. To record music, someone first sings or plays the music. The vibrations of the sounds are captured as electrical pulses and stored in a kind of electronic code on record, disk, or tape.

▲ Today's records are called compact disks, or CDs. They are smaller than old-fashioned records but hold more music.

■ How CDs are made

▼ To record music, a musician or a band plays the music, which is picked up by a microphone.

▲ The sound waves coming from the microphone are stored as electrical pulses.

Music is recorded on a CD in the form of tiny pits etched on a plastic disk. A laser reads the pits and changes what it reads into sound.

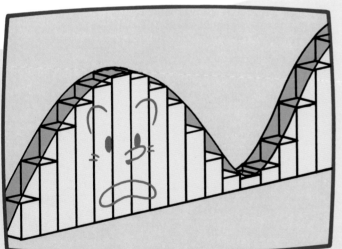

The electrical pulses of the sound waves are changed into steps. It takes a sequence of 40,000 steps to produce a single second of sound.

Instead of a continuous wave, the steps are represented by rows of symbols, similar to bar codes. This is called digital storage.

What Makes the Color in Paint?

ANSWER People have used color to paint their world since ancient times. Many colors can be made from natural materials. These materials include minerals, soil, and parts of plants and animals. The substance that gives paint its color is called a pigment.

■ Natural pigments

Rocks contain different minerals that give them their color. Some minerals, such as lead and cadmium, are ground up to make pigments.

Soil dug from the ground comes in many different colors. After the soil has been washed, it can be mixed with a paint base to color it yellow, red, brown, or even green.

The ink from a squid can be used as paint. It makes a dark brown color.

Different parts of trees, including the sap, nuts, flowers, leaves, and roots, make natural paints.

Liquid pressed from the flowers and roots of many plants can be used for coloring things.

44

■ Making colors

▲ Red paint can be made by grinding up the mineral cadmium.

▲ Orange is produced by a blend of the minerals cadmium, chromium, and lead.

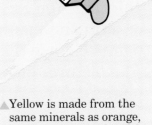

▲Yellow is made from the same minerals as orange, but they are mixed in different amounts.

▲ Green is mixed from many ingredients, including cadmium, chromium, copper, and cobalt.

▲ The ingredients in blue can come from the buckthorn plant and the elements chromium and cobalt.

▲Soil and the ink squirted by the squid are ingredients used for brown.

▲ Certain plants as well as charcoal are used for making black.

▲ Lead, zinc, and titanium are used for making white.

How Many Ways Can You Paint a Picture?

ANSWER Pencils, felt-tip markers, and crayons are some of the tools for drawing and painting. You can also dip your fingers or a brush in paint. Different tools and paints change the way a picture looks. The pictures below show the same plants drawn with different materials.

■ Pencil

▲ Pencils make drawing easy. You can erase lines to change the picture. Then you can add colors.

■ Watercolor

▲ Watercolor paints are mixed with water and applied with a brush. By adding more water, you can make the colors softer.

■ Pastels

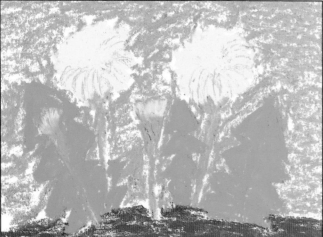

▲ Pastels are like chalk or crayons. The artist does not have to wait for the color to dry.

■ Felt-tip markers

▲ With colored markers you can make bold pictures.

■ Different brushes

Brushes come in many shapes and sizes. Thin pointed ones are best for drawing fine lines. Bigger brushes are used for painting in larger areas. Soft brushes are needed for working with watercolor paints. Stiffer brushes are used with oil or acrylic paints.

■ Mixing materials

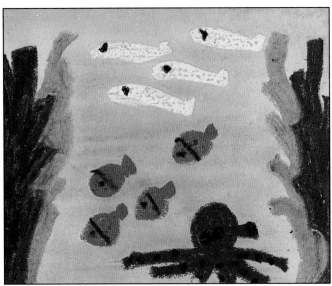

▲ This picture was drawn first with pastels. Then watercolor paints were brushed over it to create a watery effect.

▲ The bold outlines here were made with felt-tip markers. Watercolors were added later to fill in the images.

● To the Parent

Children love to experiment when drawing or painting. Depending on their age, they can be encouraged to try many different materials to express themselves. Some intriguing effects can be achieved by mixing media. If the paper is strong enough, children can try drawing into wet paint with soft pencil or oil pastels. (Pastels are chalks or crayons made of finely ground pigments. They can be purchased in art supply stores.) Children can also draw over oil pastels or mix soft pastels with watercolors and paint.

How Is Pottery Made?

ANSWER

Pottery is made from clay, which comes from the ground. The potter first squeezes and presses the clay to make it softer. He or she shapes the clay to form a pot. Then the pot must be dried. Clay can be formed with the hands alone. Or it can be placed on a potter's wheel and shaped while spinning around. Sometimes clay is poured into a mold to make a pot.

This building is made in the adobe style of Native Americans of the southwestern United States. The bricks are formed from clay mixed with straw. Adobe bricks are dried in the sun.

How a bowl is made

1 A potter places a lump of clay on a potter's wheel and shapes the clay into a bowl.

2 The potter sets the finished bowl aside to let it dry.

3 The dried bowl is then baked at a high temperature in an oven called a kiln.

4 Next the potter dips the pot in a coating called a glaze. The glaze can also be put on by brushing or spraying.

5 The potter sets the bowl aside to let the glaze dry.

6 Finally, the glazed pot is again baked, or fired, at a higher temperature. The pot comes out with a shiny finish.

■ Pit firing

Shaping the clay

Drying before baking

▷ Pots can also be fired in a pit lined with stones. The pots are placed inside, and a fire is lit on top.

■ Hand building

Some potters begin by making a flat base and adding coils of clay to the outside to shape the pot.

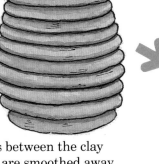

Gaps between the clay coils are smoothed away by hand.

The flattened clay is bent into shapes.

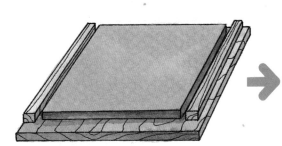

Another way to hand build is to flatten the clay on a board.

■ Adding a handle

Sometimes making pottery requires extra steps. Here a handle for a mug is shaped separately and pasted on.

● **To the Parent**

Artists have made pottery for thousands of years. The potter begins with damp clay, which is kneaded to make it pliable, then shaped. When dried and fired, it becomes hard and durable. Glazing was introduced to make pottery watertight, but it is also important for decoration.

? What Kinds of Pottery Are There?

ANSWER Clay is not all the same. Some clays have other materials mixed into them. That changes the way the clay hardens and looks when it is fired. The three main kinds of pottery are earthenware and stoneware made from potter's clay and porcelain made from china clay.

■ Stoneware

Clay mixed with other materials is baked at a high temperature. In Japan's prized Bizen ware, ashes and smoke create special patterns in the surface during firing.

▲ Ancient earthenware pot

■ Earthenware

This is the oldest kind of pottery. The first clay pots were molded by hand and dried in the sun. When fired in a kiln, an earthenware pot becomes waterproof.

▲ Bizen ware

▲ 2,000-year-old pot

Porcelain bowl

■ Porcelain

Porcelain is made from special china clay that is glazed before firing. It is fired at temperatures between 2,375° and 2,750° Fahrenheit, higher than for any other pottery.

▲ Porcelain vase

▲ A glaze can be applied to stoneware to decorate the surface and make it smooth and shiny.

▲ Vase from ancient Greece

●To the Parent

Earthenware pottery dates back 9,000 years and is still made today. Stoneware and porcelain were developed much later in China. In each case, powdered minerals are mixed with clay and fired at very high temperatures. While the clay holds its shape during firing, the minerals liquefy and harden again, giving the pottery its durable, nonporous properties. Although it can sometimes be difficult to distinguish between them, stoneware is heavier and more opaque than porcelain. In all pottery making the proper blend of materials, skillful molding by a potter, and firing at the correct temperature are essential for success.

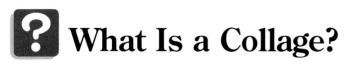

What Is a Collage?

ANSWER A collage is a picture made from scraps of paper and odd bits of things that are pasted together. You can make a collage from materials you find around your house. Try it with wallpaper, old holiday cards, and magazine pictures. If you like, you can then draw on your collage.

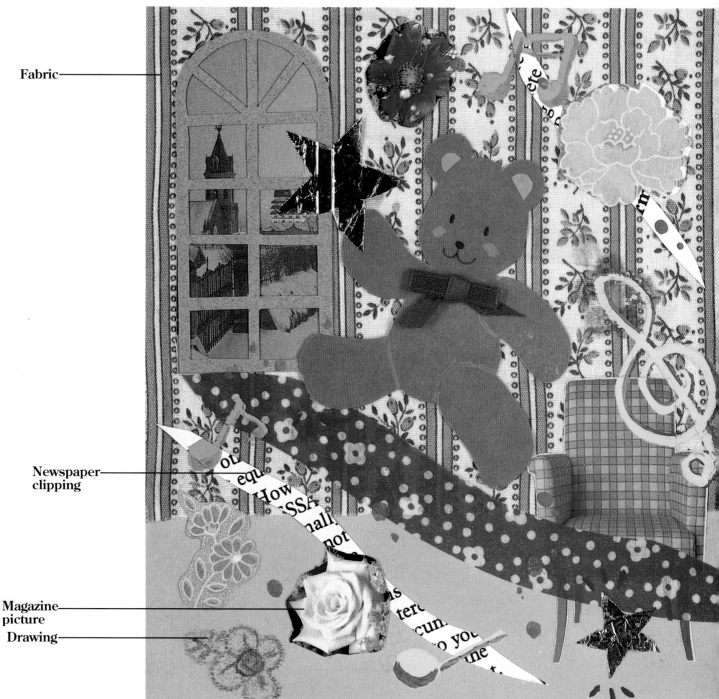

Fabric

Newspaper clipping

Magazine picture

Drawing

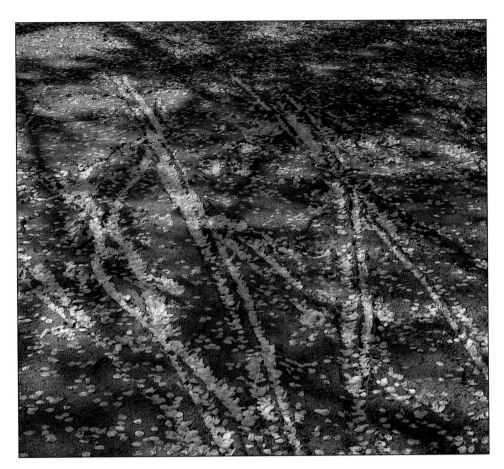

■ Street art

Sometimes a street becomes a kind of collage. The colors and textures of flower petals or fallen leaves can create a design like a work of art.

▼ An artist's collage:
Postcard Mural 5 by John Laudenslager

Postcard Mural V   Laudenslager 1986

How Can Dots Make a Picture?

ANSWER When they are all spread out, dots just look like dots. But if you place them close together, they start to look like lines and solid shapes. When you put two or more colors together in a pattern of dots, they look like a new color to your eyes. By carefully filling shapes with dots, you can create a picture.

■ Painted with dots

This picture is made of many dots placed very close together. By the skillful use of red, blue, yellow, and black, the artist created the impression of many other colors.

▲ *Sunday Afternoon on La Grande Jatte,* **by Georges Seurat**

■ Television pictures

Look closely at a television screen and you may see tiny dots of red, blue, and green. When you look at the television screen from farther away, your eyes mix the dots and you see a full-color picture.

■ Newspaper pictures

Photographs in newspapers and magazines are also made up of dots. Try looking at a newspaper picture through a magnifying glass. Can you see how dots make a picture?

Why Are There So Many Different Styles of Art in the World?

(ANSWER) Artists have made pictures since ancient times. From one part of the world to another, people developed their own ways of drawing, painting, and sculpting. Every piece of art says a lot about the place where it came from and the people who made it.

▶ In ancient Egypt, wall paintings were made to record important events.

■ Art around the world

◀ A painting with a calendar on top, painted in Europe in the Middle Ages, shows how people lived and farmed.

▶ Ancient Greece is famous for its sculptures, such as this one called *Winged Victory of Samothrace*. Most of these statues have been damaged over time, but people still marvel at their beauty.

◀ A wood-block print made in Japan shows famous Mount Fuji in the distance through the dip in the waves.

▲ A Chinese picture of a
landscape was drawn with
India ink.

◀ This Buddhist sculpture was
made in India. The statue's
clothing is typical of India's
clothing in ancient times.

▲ A sculpted stone calendar
shows the artistic style of
Mexico's Aztec people.

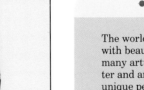

▲ **A ritual mask from Africa**

●To the Parent

The world's museums are filled
with beautiful works of art. In
many artworks the subject mat-
ter and artistic style reflect the
unique perspective of a particular culture. Powerful styles also
inspire artists in other cultures
to incorporate those elements
into their own work. For in-
stance, ancient Greek sculpture
influenced the artist who made
the Gandhara Buddhist sculpture pictured above.

 What Is Sculpture?

ANSWER Unlike paintings, which are flat, a sculpture is an object of art that has dimension. Sculptures can be made out of stone, wood, paper, metal, or even ice. The sandcastle you build at the beach is a kind of sculpture. Sculptures sometimes look like real people or things, but they can also look like something from an artist's imagination.

■ Wood sculpture

Totem poles are carved out of wood by Native Americans living in the northwestern part of the United States and Canada. The main part of this totem pole was carved out of a single tree trunk. The wings were carved separately and attached later. The figures are different spirits that are important in the Native American culture.

■ Stone sculpture

A hammer and chisel are the main tools used to carve a figure out of a hard material like stone. Stone sculptures, like this lion, often decorate gardens. This one lies quietly in a garden in Antibes, France.

■ Metal sculpture

This large metal sculpture was created by American sculptor Alexander Calder in 1969. It is made out of painted steel plate and stands about 31 feet tall. Because Calder liked to use this shade of red in his sculptures, the color is known as Calder red. The name of this imaginative sculpture is *Hats Off*. Many people think they see a person or an animal or both when they look at it. What do you see?

■ Ice sculpture

Sculptures can also be carved out of blocks of ice. They are beautiful while they last! This sculpture of a swan was part of a competition held in Rochester, Minnesota. People from all over the world come here each winter to carve sculptures from ice.

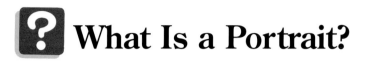

What Is a Portrait?

(ANSWER) A portrait is a picture of someone. It can be just a face or a whole body. Long ago there were no cameras for taking photographs or videos. Portraits were the only way to keep a visual record of the way people looked. At first, only people of importance, like kings and queens and other members of royalty, had their portraits done. But later, artists began painting portraits of ordinary people, like farmers and merchants.

■ Portraits over the years

Portrait of Battista Sforza by Piero della Francesca (Italian). A profile is a drawing of the face from the side. Most early portraits, like this one done around 1465, were profiles. This is how faces on coins usually appear.

Mona Lisa by Leonardo da Vinci (Italian). This is one of the most famous portraits ever painted. It was painted about 40 years after the one on the left. You see a little more of the woman's body. And her face, which is looking at you, has a much more relaxed expression.

Portrait of a Woman by Frans Hals (Dutch). In the 17th century artists began to paint portraits of ordinary people, not just important people. Frans Hals painted this portrait and similar works from 1630 to 1650.

Nelly O'Brien by Sir Joshua Reynolds (English). Portrait painting developed more in the 18th century. This portrait, painted in 1761, shows almost the whole body of a young woman with a very charming expression on her face.

■ Make a portrait

Try drawing a picture of yourself. This is called a self-portrait. First look at your face in a mirror. What is the basic shape of your face? Is it oval or is it round? Draw the shape on a piece of paper. Follow the diagram at the right to add your eyes, nose, and mouth.

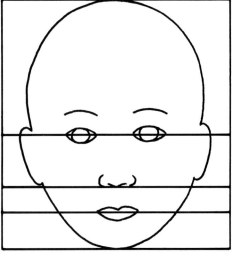

Your eyes are about halfway between the top of your head and your chin. Your nose is halfway between your eyes and chin, and your mouth is halfway between your nose and chin.

? What Is a Paper Print?

ANSWER A paper print is a picture made by pressing a piece of paper over paper shapes that have been covered with ink. The ink on the shapes sticks to the paper to create an ink picture of the shapes. Sometimes the shapes form a picture of something, and sometimes they just make an interesting pattern.

1 A paper print begins with an idea. The shapes needed for a picture of this idea are then cut out of thick paper. Simple shapes work best.

■ Making a paper print

2 Next, the shapes are pasted down carefully to form the picture on a heavy piece of paper. This piece of paper becomes the printing plate.

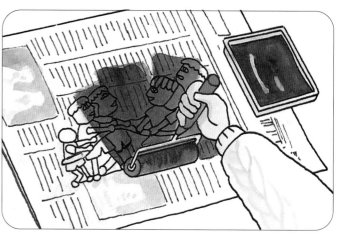

3 A special tool called a brayer is rolled in ink. A thin, even layer of ink is rolled over the picture on the printing plate.

4 A piece of paper is carefully placed on top of the inked picture. The paper is rubbed with a small pad to press it against the printing plate.

5 When the paper is lifted off, the print of the picture appears in reverse. Printing is a way to make many copies of the same picture.

■ Making a stencil

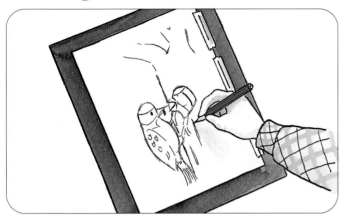

1 Another way to make many copies of a picture is by using a stencil. First, a picture is outlined on a piece of paper. Large, simple shapes work best. There also must be a border so the picture will not fall apart when cut out.

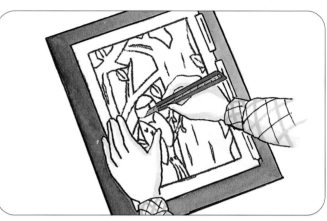

2 When the drawing is finished, the insides of the shapes are cut out to create a stencil. The stencil is then taped onto a piece of drawing paper so that it will not slip.

3 Next, paint is added. It is dabbed over the picture using a brush, a piece of cloth, or a sponge. The paint goes through the "windows" in the stencil and creates an image of the shapes on the paper.

4 When the dabbing is finished, the stencil is carefully removed. The picture appears on the paper below. Once the stencil is dry, it can be used again. When the stencil is turned over, an opposite picture can be made.

◄ **A stencil print**

● **To the Parent**

Paper prints and stencils can be fun to make. An image that can be printed over and over can be used by a child as a party invitation or a thank-you note. To achieve the best results, younger children will need some supervision with certain steps. Let your child choose and draw a subject, making sure it is a fairly simple image. In the case of stencil making, cutting presents a particular challenge. You may wish to cut out your child's picture using an X-Acto knife. In that case, the picture can be drawn on a heavier paper stock so the finished stencil will last longer.

What Is Origami?

ANSWER Origami is the art of folding paper. Usually without any cutting or pasting, paper is folded to make beautiful objects such as birds, fish, boats, figures, and flowers. Colorful patterned papers are sometimes used to make origami even more attractive.

■ Make an origami boat

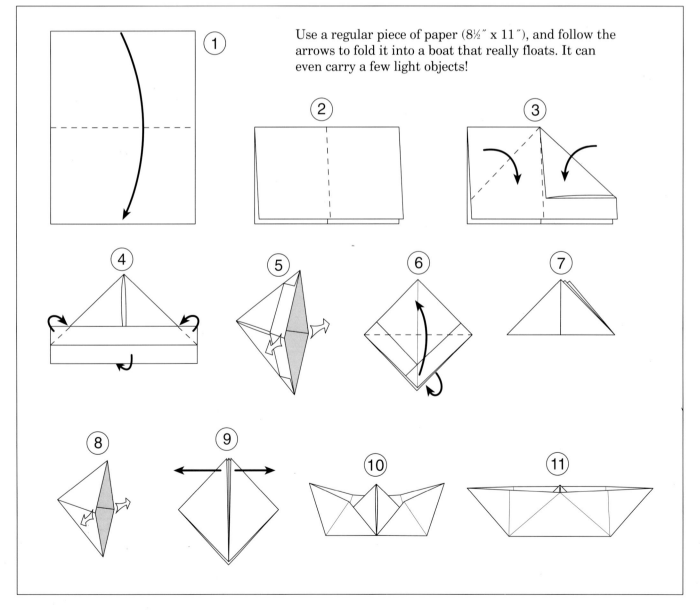

Use a regular piece of paper (8½″ x 11″), and follow the arrows to fold it into a boat that really floats. It can even carry a few light objects!

■ Make a paper dog

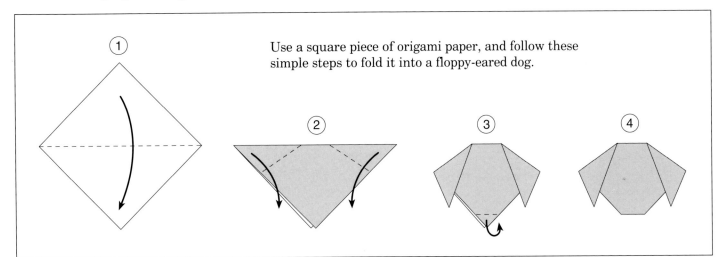

①
Use a square piece of origami paper, and follow these simple steps to fold it into a floppy-eared dog.

② ③ ④

■ A land of paper animals

A skilled origami artist can fold colorful paper into intricate shapes like the animals in this picture. Some of these figures required more than 50 folds to complete.

● To the Parent

The craft of folding paper into objects has been practiced in Asia for centuries. The best known and most sophisticated is the Japanese art of origami, which still has ceremonial and decorative uses in that country. At its most elaborate, origami may require hundreds of folds to make an object. Step-by-step directions for two simpler examples are also shown for children who want to try some origami. Even the easier designs require a certain amount of skill and patience to master.

How Can Things Look Far Away on a Flat Piece of Paper?

(ANSWER) When you look at a flat drawing, some things seem to be closer to you than others. This is just like the real world. But the real world is not flat. Artists have learned ways of making their drawings look like what our eyes see. One trick they use is called perspective. You can use this artist's trick in your drawings, too.

■ **This looks wrong!**

Look carefully at this drawing. The man who is farther away looks much too big. In real life, things that are farther away look smaller.

■ **This looks right!**

Here is a similar scene using perspective. The man in the distance appears much smaller. The buildings in the distance also look smaller.

■ Lines from one point

When lines are added to this drawing, you can see that they all meet at one point. This point is called a vanishing point. To draw things in the distance, first decide where you want the vanishing point to be in your picture. Then draw lines stretching out from it. Use these lines as guides when you draw buildings. They will help your picture look more realistic.

■ Lines from two points

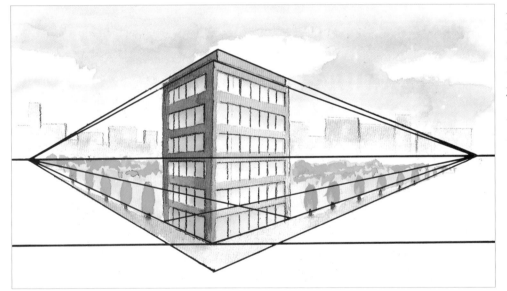

A picture can have two vanishing points instead of one. In this case the vanishing points appear on the left and right and seem far away. In a picture like this, you also need to establish a horizon line. This is the line where the sky meets the land. Choosing a horizon line changes the perspective, as you can see below.

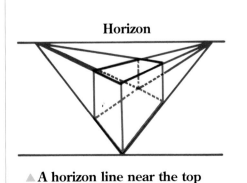

Horizon

▲ A horizon line near the top

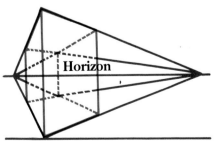

Horizon

▲ A horizon line in the middle

● **To the Parent**

Showing distance on a flat surface is called perspective. Making one spot the focal, or vanishing, point of a picture gives the picture the appearance of depth. When two focal points are used to give depth to both sides of a picture, it is known as two-point perspective. These techniques are hard for young children to understand. You may wish to suggest to them that things drawn larger and closer to the bottom of the page will appear nearer in their pictures.

How Are Cartoons Made?

(ANSWER) Although they seem to move, cartoons are made from still pictures. To create a cartoon, an artist draws many pictures of the same character. Each picture looks almost identical to the next, but there is a small change. When you see them quickly one after another, your eye blends the pictures together. This makes the character appear to move.

▲ For cartoons to work, you must see many pictures very quickly. Every second of a television cartoon, you are seeing 24 slightly different pictures, one right after the other.

■ Fooling your eyes

Something that fools your eyes is called an optical illusion. This illusion uses a card with a picture of a horse on one side and a picture of a rider on the other side. When you spin the card, your eyes see both images and your brain puts them together. Your eyes are fooled into thinking they see the rider sitting on the horse.

■ Make your own cartoon

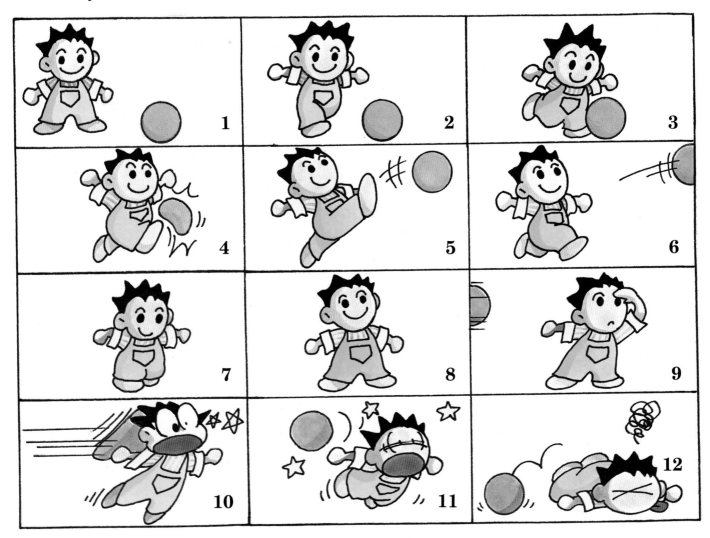

Copy or trace each of these drawings. Cut them out, stack them in order, and clip them together on one side. When you flip through them, it will look as if the boy is kicking the ball. Try to make other flip books using your own ideas.

●To the Parent

A characteristic of the human eye is that it retains images for a moment after a picture is no longer visible. Animation relies on this so-called afterimage to make a series of images with very subtle changes appear to be moving when shown in rapid succession. In 1878 Eadweard Muybridge, an Englishman who pioneered animation, used a series of rapidly shot photographs of a galloping horse to show that all four feet are off the ground at one point. Three years later he invented the zoopraxiscope, a forerunner of the motion picture projector.

How Can You Use Simple Shapes to Draw Pictures?

(ANSWER) Most objects are made up of basic shapes like circles and squares. Sometimes you have to look closely to see these shapes. It is easier to draw an object if you start with the shapes it is made of.

▲ A ball is a circle.

■ Look for the shape

Before you start to draw an object, look at it carefully. Does it have one main shape like the can, the ball, and the television set you see here?

▲ A can is a cylinder.

▲ A television set is box shaped.

■ Find the hidden shapes

Sometimes it is hard to see the shapes right away, so you must study the object closely. You may even find that it is made of more than one shape.

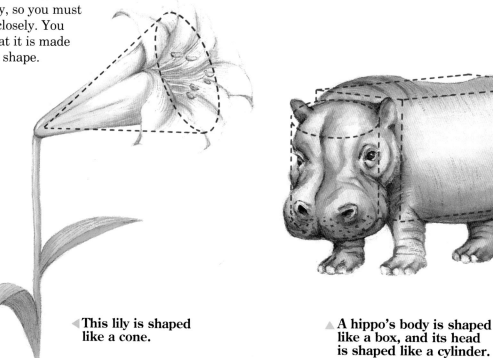

◁ This lily is shaped like a cone.

▲ A hippo's body is shaped like a box, and its head is shaped like a cylinder.

■ The shape of a house

If you look closely at this house, you will see many different shapes mixed together. Can you find a triangle and a rectangle?

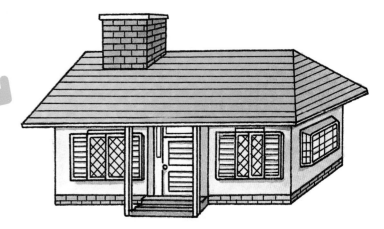

▲ To draw a house, start with a box that is shaped like a rectangle. The roof is made from a trapezoid and a triangle.

▲ After you draw your basic shapes, you can add things like windows and doors to make your picture look more real.

TRY THIS

■ Drawing a cat

What different shapes go into drawing a cat? You can see them in the picture below.

▲ The head has the shape of a ball, and the body has the shape of a cylinder.

▲ The shapes are smoothed together, and shadows and color are added to finish the drawing.

● **To the Parent**

Every solid object has a basic shape. Try showing your child different things around the house and asking what shapes he or she sees. Your child can then try to draw the objects. For younger children, shapes with volume such as spheres and cylinders are difficult to draw. Children may be more comfortable working with flat shapes such as circles and squares.

Why Do Some Artists Paint Such Unusual-Looking Pictures?

(ANSWER) Many artists paint pictures that look real, the way photographs do. Other artists paint in different ways. They do not want to show the world as it appears. Instead they use colors, shapes, and lines to express their ideas and feelings. This type of art is called modern art.

▲ This painting by Russian artist Wassily Kandinsky is called *Ribbon with Squares*. What do you see here?

▶ This painting by Spanish artist Joan Miró is called *A Man and His Dog in the Sun*. Can you see why he gave it that name?

More modern artists

The paintings on this page show the work of three famous modern artists. In the 1800s, Vincent van Gogh painted with swirling colors and bold brush strokes. In this century, Henri Matisse and Pablo Picasso created images out of vivid shapes and bright colors.

▲ *The Starry Night,* by Vincent van Gogh

▲ *The Sadness of the King,* by Henri Matisse

▲ *Woman Weeping,* by Pablo Picasso

How Can Pictures Be Made from a Block of Wood?

ANSWER Wood-block prints are made by using a sharp tool to cut a picture into a block of wood. When paint is brushed on the block, it covers only those areas that have not been cut out. A piece of paper is pressed onto the wood, touching the block everywhere except where cuts were made. When the paper is peeled off, the picture appears as white lines because there is no paint where the picture is.

■ How one is made

▲ First a picture is drawn on a piece of paper with a pencil.

▲ Then a mirror image of the picture is copied in ink onto a block of wood.

▲ The artist follows the ink lines to cut out the picture with a sharp tool.

■ Careful cutter

Wood-block gouges are sharp, like knives. Artists have to be very careful when they use them. The block is steadied with one hand and cut with the other. The artist keeps both hands behind the sharp tool to avoid accidents.

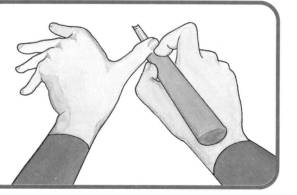

■ Many blades

To cut a picture out of wood, an artist must use a sharp tool called a gouge. Gouges come with different blades to make different shapes. Here you can see the kinds of cuts some of these blades make.

1 Slanted blade **2** U gouge **3** V gouge **4** Flat gouge

▲ After the wood block is cut, ink is rolled onto it lightly and evenly.

▲ Paper is carefully placed on top of the inked block and rubbed with a small pad.

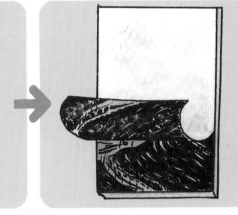

▲ The finished print is then carefully lifted from the wood block.

■ A good work surface

Artists who make wood-block prints often have a special, flat work surface that fits over a tabletop. This keeps the block from slipping.

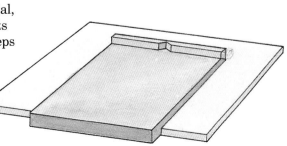

 What Is Marbling?

(ANSWER) Marbling is a way to make lovely swirling patterns on paper. They are made from oil paint that is poured into water. The paint and water do not mix. Instead, they make beautiful designs. These designs look like the patterns in a kind of rock called marble, which is how this art got its name.

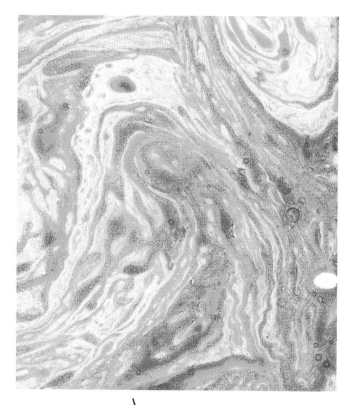

▷ Marbling prints are made by swirling oil paint into water.

■ Marbling

Fill a shallow dish or pan with water. Gently dribble oil paint into the water.

Stir the paint slowly with a stick, or drag a comb from side to side and front to back.

(CHECK IT OUT)

To marble only part of a sheet of paper, hold one edge out of the water. Be sure to keep it still while the oil-paint pattern soaks onto the part of the paper where you want it.

Once the marbling pattern has dried, you can use crayons, pastels, or other drawing materials to add to your picture. When you are finished, be sure to give your picture a name.

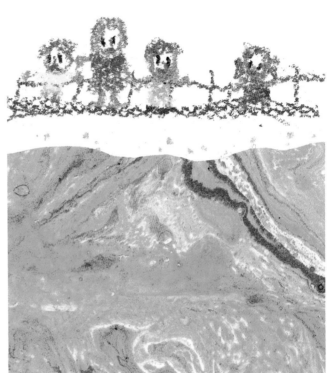

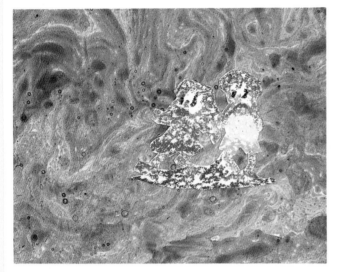

▲ *The Magical Country*

▲ *Suspension Bridge*

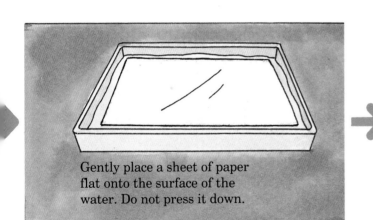

Gently place a sheet of paper flat onto the surface of the water. Do not press it down.

Let the paper soak up the oil paint. Now, remove the paper and let it dry.

● **To the Parent**

Marbling is a process for creating unusual and interesting visual patterns by dropping oil paint into water in a shallow pan. Younger children who are not yet able to master the delicate technique needed to marble paper might want to try a simpler process. A parent can use a blunt knife to scrape different-colored chalk particles onto the surface of water in a shallow pan. Then, the child can lay a piece of paper gently onto the surface. As with the oil paint, the chalk particles will adhere to the paper to create interesting, swirly patterns.

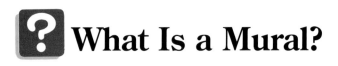

What Is a Mural?

ANSWER A mural is a picture painted or drawn on a wall or a ceiling. There are many ways to make murals. Sometimes an artist paints right on a wall. Other artists paint on wet plaster. When the plaster dries, the painting becomes part of the wall.

■ A neighborhood mural

In the neighborhoods of many cities and towns, brightly colored murals have been painted on walls and buildings. These murals frequently show pictures of people and events that are im-

portant to the community. The mural shown above, entitled *Tribute to Life,* is in Washington, D.C., and was painted by 20 young students under the guidance of muralist Jorge Somarriba. The colorful mural measures 600 feet long and took three summers to complete.

78

■ A ceiling mural

One of the most famous murals in the world is the one on the ceiling of the Sistine Chapel at the Vatican in Rome. It was painted by Italian artist Michelangelo between 1508 and 1512. This kind of mural is called a fresco. Fresco means "fresh" in Italian. Instead of painting right on the ceiling, Michelangelo first put down fresh, wet plaster and then painted on the plaster. When the plaster dried, the paints became permanent. To paint the ceiling, the great painter had to lie on his back on a scaffold 60 feet above the floor. He did this for four years before the fresco was completed.

● To the Parent

Mural painting is an ancient means of artistic expression in which walls or ceilings are treated like huge canvases and are decorated. Cave paintings in Spain and France are the earliest known murals. The art form progressed through many civilizations, including ancient Egypt and Greece. During the Renaissance, fresco painting supplanted mosaics as the mural style of choice. In the 20th century, Diego Rivera and other Mexican muralists painted murals to express revolutionary themes with great effectiveness.

What Are These?

▼ This unusual-looking instrument is called a harp piano. It has a keyboard like a piano, but it produces a sound similar to that of a harp.

▲ With its cover on, a stick violin looks like a walking stick. When the cover is removed, you can see how it looks like a violin.

◄ This music box looks like a piano mounted sideways on a cart. It plays music when you turn the handle.

Growing-Up Album

Which Belong to the Same Group?

In the top row are four musical instruments that produce sounds in different ways. Can you match each of these instruments to the one in the bottom row that produces sounds the same way?

A. Harmonica

B. Recorder

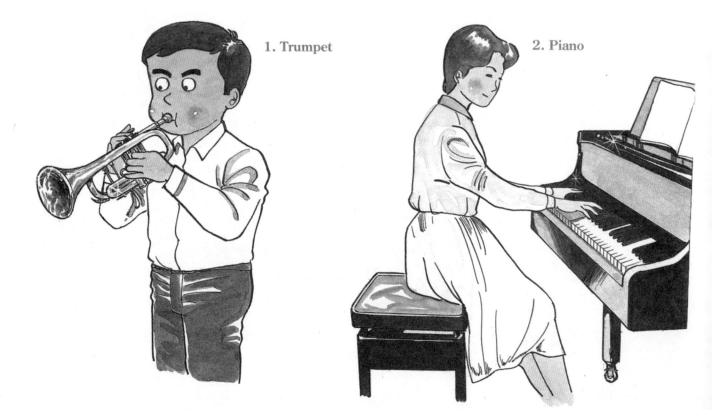

1. Trumpet

2. Piano

C. Drum

D. Violin

3. Accordion

4. Cymbals

Answers: (A)-(3), (B)-(1), (C)-(4), (D)-(2).

Which Led to Each Instrument?

On the top of the page are four instruments from long ago. Each led to the development of a modern instrument shown at the bottom of the page. Can you match each old instrument to a modern one?

A

B

C

D

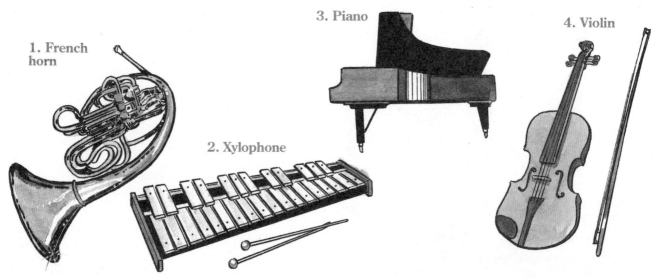

1. French horn

2. Xylophone

3. Piano

4. Violin

Answers: (A)-(1), (B)-(2), (C)-(3), (D)-(4).

What Kind of Print Are We Making?

What kind of print will you get if you use the method shown in the steps on this page? Choose your answer from among the three finished prints shown in the square below.

1. Cut out shapes from thick paper, and paste them onto a piece of paper to make a picture. You now have a printing plate.

2. Put ink over the printing plate with a special roller called a brayer.

3. Cover the plate with a piece of paper, and rub it with a small pad.

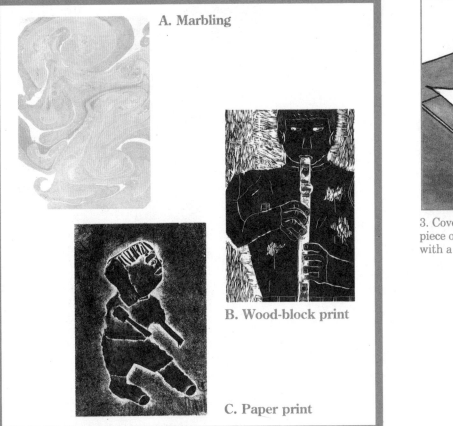

A. Marbling

B. Wood-block print

C. Paper print

Answer: C. Paper print.

Which Was Used to Draw Each Picture?

On the right are four different drawing tools. Each was used to make one of the pictures below. Can you match each tool to the picture it made?

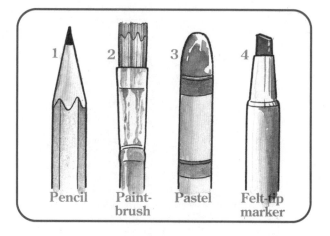

1 Pencil
2 Paint-brush
3 Pastel
4 Felt-tip marker

A

B

C

D

Answers: (1)-(D), (2)-(B), (3)-(A), (4)-(C).

Which Picture Was Drawn Using One-Point Perspective?

Each picture on this page shows a street scene. One picture uses a vanishing point to give it perspective. Can you find it?

Answer: 2.

A Child's First Library of Learning

Staff for
MUSIC AND ART

Editorial Directors: Jean Burke Crawford, Karin Kinney
Editorial Coordinator: Marike van der Veen
Editorial Assistant: Mary M. Saxton
Production Manager: Marlene Zack
Copyeditors: Donna D. Carey, Heidi A. Fritschel
Picture Coordinator: David A. Herod
Quality Assurance Manager: Miriam P. Newton
Library: Louise D. Forstall
Computer Composition: Janet Barnes Syring
Design/Illustration: Antonio Alcalá, John Jackson,
    David Neal Wiseman
Special contributor: Andrew Gutelle (text)
Photography/Illustration: Cover: Photography by JoAnn
    Simmons-Swing. Back cover: Courtesy The Beauvoir School,
    Washington, D.C. 1: Courtesy The Beauvoir School,
    Washington, D.C. 6: Art by Linda Greigg (middle left). 7: Art
    by Linda Greigg (bottom right). 8: Art by Linda Greigg (bot-
    tom). 13: Art by Linda Greigg (bottom left). 21: Art by Linda
    Greigg (top left); JoAnn Simmons-Swing (3 photos of chil-
    dren). 22: Art by Linda Greigg (bottom right). 24: Art by
    Linda Greigg (bottom left). 25: Art by Linda Greigg (computer
    chip). 26: Art by Fred Holz; photo courtesy National
    Symphony Orchestra, photography by Donna Cantor-
    Maclean. 32: Art by Linda Greigg. 55: Art by Fred Holz (news-
    paper lower left). 58: © Adins Tovy/The Stock Shop (top left);
    © Gilles Vauclair/The Stock Shop (bottom right). 59: © H. G.
    Ross/The Stock Shop (bottom left); © Irving Shapiro/The
    Stock Shop (top right). 61: Art by Linda Greigg (bottom
    right). 65: Art by John Drummond (except child). 71: © Clyde
    H. Smith/The Stock Shop (top right). 78: JoAnn Simmons-
    Swing, courtesy DC Art/Works, Washington, D.C. (bottom
    left); © Rick Reinhard, courtesy Latin American Youth
    Center, Washington, D. C. (top right). 79: Scala/Art
    Resource, New York.
Overread: Barbara Klein
Consultants: David Brundage (music), Suzanne Weidie (art)

Library of Congress Cataloging-in-Publication Data
Music and art.
    p.   cm. – (A Child's First Library of Learning)
    ISBN 0-8094-9474-4 (hardcover)
    ISBN 0-8094-9475-2 (library)
    1. Musical instruments—Juvenile literature. 2. Music—
    Acoustics and physics—Juvenile literature. 3. Art—Juvenile
    literature. [1. Musical instruments. 2. Music. 3. Art.]
I. Time-Life Books. II. Series.
ML460.M947 1994
700—dc20   94-2318
                                                    CIP
                                            AC MN

TIME-LIFE for CHILDREN ®

Managing Editor: Patricia Daniels
Editorial Directors: Jean Burke Crawford, Allan Fallow,
    Karin Kinney, Sara Mark
Senior Art Director: Sue White
Editorial Coordinator: Marike van der Veen
Editorial Assistant: Mary M. Saxton

Original English translation by International Editorial Services
Inc./C. E. Berry

First printing. Printed in U.S.A.
Published simultaneously in Canada.

Time-Life Books is a division of TIME LIFE INC.

TIME-LIFE is a trademark of Time Warner Inc. U.S.A.

School and library distribution by Time-Life Education,
P.O. Box 85026, Richmond, Virginia 23285-5026.
For subscription information, call 1-800-621-7026.

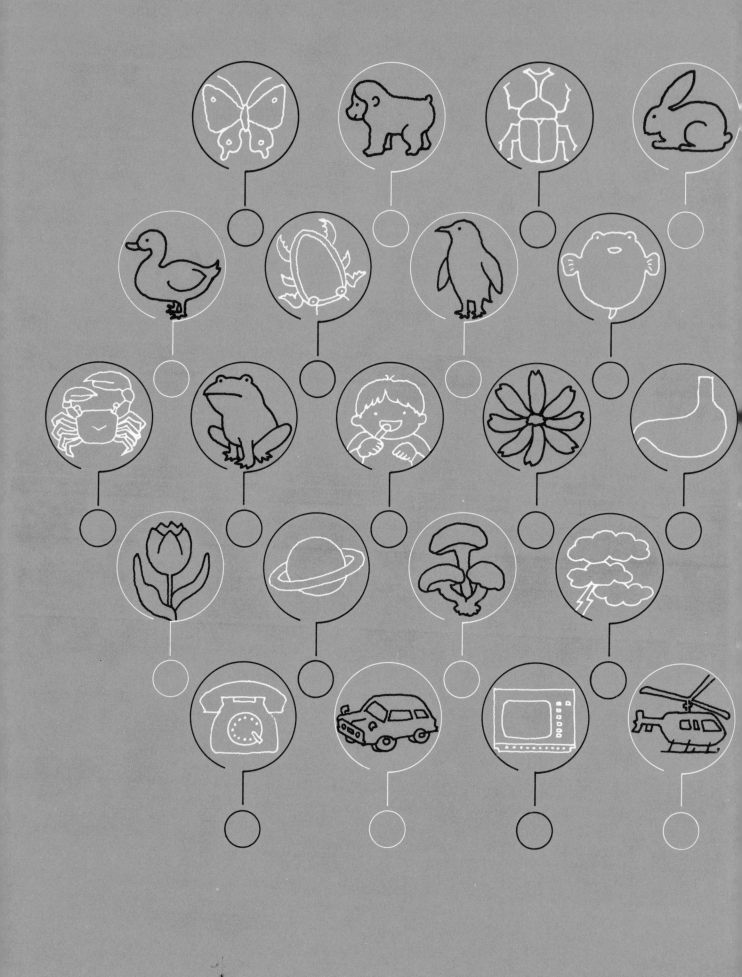